SWITZERLAND FOR BEGINNERS

SWITZERLAND
for beginners

GEORGE MIKES

Illustrated by Godi Hofmann

Revised and enlarged edition

ANDRE DEUTSCH

This edition published February 1975 by
André Deutsch Limited
105 Great Russell Street London WC1
Second impression June 1976
Third impression July 1978
Fourth impression May 1981
Fifth impression November 1982
Sixth impression February 1985

Printed and bound in Great Britain by
Redwood Burn Limited
Trowbridge, Wiltshire

ISBN 0 233 96621 8

*To my son, Martin,
who lives in Switzerland
and is no beginner*

CONTENTS

Preface

This little book was originally written partly at the request of my Swiss publisher and partly at the request of Radio Basle. It first appeared in German and — how does that impressive pseudo-modest English phrase go? — it was not altogether a failure.

It is as the result of heavy and unrelenting pressure that it now appears in my adopted mother-tongue, too. It was I who exerted the pressure; it was my publisher who succumbed to it.

The piece on Liechtenstein first appeared in *Encounter* in 1958. It is a piece I am especially proud of as it fulfilled a long dream of mine.

I had always hoped to be the centre of a resounding international storm because of something I had written. In my mind's eye I often saw a dictator shaking his fist at me; or angry questions being asked in the parliament of one democracy or another, accompanied by furious uproar from the extreme right; vituperative articles attacking me in the nationalist Press, crying out for my blood. And there I would stand, right in the middle of the international arena, shaking my head with quiet determination — a superior smile on my lips. 'Out of the question!' I heard myself reply. 'I shall *not* withdraw that particular joke; I *did* mean every word of that anecdote, and meant it in deadly earnest.'

My dream, alas, faded as time went on. People, instead of drawing their swords or throwing plastic bombs into my flat, patted me on the back and said,

'Quite amusing.' It is true that I was once challenged to a duel by an Italian patriot; but he, too, having challenged me, sat down to read my book, *Italy for Beginners,* quite liked it and now we are devoted and lifelong friends. So I was about to bury a cherished dream when Liechtenstein came to the rescue.

The *Liechtensteiner Volksblatt* — the *Times* of Liechtenstein, which appears practically every other day — launched an attack upon my tactlessness. The real reason for this attack was that an article had appeared in the *Ostschweizer Zeitung,* giving the widest possible publicity to my article on Liechtenstein. Perhaps the world at large does not read the *Ostschweizer Zeitung*; but — what is much more important — the whole of St Gallen does. The reply of the *Liechtensteiner Volksblatt* could hardly be called vitriolic; but its author was obviously angry, roused and pained, and this gave me great satisfaction. As no special committee of the US Senate ever discussed any chapters of *How to Scrape Skies*; no special session of the French House of Deputies was called after the appearance of *Little Cabbages*; and the imperturbable Japanese remained as imperturbed as ever after the publication of *East is East*,* the wrath of Liechtenstein will have to do for me.

Perhaps that's the right size for me.

In any case, my gratitude will be everlasting.

London, April 1962   G.M.

---

*And after *The Land of the Rising Yen,* too: doubly disappointing, since it was my second shot at them.

Preface to the Revised and Enlarged Edition

As the late Sam Goldwyn put it in his own immortal way: we have passed a lot of water since I wrote the first preface to this book, twelve years ago. *Switzerland for Beginners* has been reprinted four times, and interest in it — amazingly but gratifyingly — is still alive. But it is not only I — and you, Gentle Reader — who have changed in these twelve years: Switzerland has changed a little too. Not the basic Swiss character, Swiss virtues and vices, of course, but some of the details. To the xeno-phobia between Zürich and Basle, between Aarau and Winterthur, has been added the xenophobia between the Swiss and the *Gastarbeiter* — guest workers, as foreign labourers are somewhat euphemistically called. Women have received the vote, though Switzerland has not exactly been turned into one of the flagbearers of Women's Lib. To cut a long story short, a few new chap-ters had to be added to this book. Others had to be brought up to date, some statements had to be corrected, a few opinions and data had to be slightly revised. I have also taken the opportunity of adding a chapter or two on subjects which might have been dealt with in the original edition but were not. For example: on the Gnomes of Zürich and on the fascinating problem of Switzerland's fourth language, Romansch, and the even more fascinating art of yodelling.

This little book was kindly received by my Swiss friends and my Swiss enemies: not surprising, because in spite of its leg-pulling it must be obvious to all that I

love Switzerland, indeed regard her as my second —
well, to be precise, my third — country. From the first,
Hungary, I have been expelled and I cannot — and do
not wish to — return. My second home, Britain, I
love more and more, the more decadent and hopeless she
gets, which means that, by now, my love has become a
mad passion. But Switzerland, where my son lives, is
the country which I visit most often and stay in with
the most pleasure. To my surprise, the one thing to
which my Swiss friends objected was that I called them
money-minded — indeed, slightly on the close-fisted side.
This seemed to me as if Nigerians had asked me re-
proachfully: 'Do you really think we are black?' Or
Americans: 'You really don't see that our children are
the best brought-up in the world?'

A few days ago the most recent objector, a Swiss
writer, put it this way: 'All the people in the world are
money-minded — why pick on us? Besides, the whole
world loves the Swiss franc, why shouldn't we?' The love
of money, alas, is almost — thank God, not quite —
universal. People rob banks, commit frauds, speculate
and devise honest and dishonest means to become millionaires. Others scheme to make two million dollars or
a hundred and fifty thousand pounds. The Swiss alone
worry about fifty-five centimes. Yes, the whole world
loves the Swiss franc; but only the Swiss adore the Swiss
centime.

Finally, I must report one of the great disappoint-
ments of my life. I returned to Liechtenstein, to revise
that chapter. I was received by the Prince and Princess (separately) and both, most kindly, remember-
ed my original little piece on their country and quoted
from it. They said they had enjoyed it. Naturally this
was very gratifying, since I had never intended to offend
that charming and tiny country. But what happens now
to my heroic pose, my defiance, my self-esteem if even

the *Liechtensteiner Volksblatt* stops disapproving of me?

London, April 1974   G.M.

The Largest Country
in the World

One of the best guarded secrets of the Swiss is that there are really no such people. There are no Swiss. The outside world may be misled by superficial external appearances; the Swiss themselves — for reasons of policy, diplomacy and also because it would be too complicated to explain all this to dense foreigners — refrain from destroying the legend and behave as though they existed. But they do not.

Looking at the map you might easily jump to the conclusion that the United States is a larger country than Switzerland. Wrong again. It is much smaller. This is one of the reasons why you can speak of 'Americans' but you cannot really speak of 'the Swiss'. In the United States quite a lot of people, whether from the Wild West (Oregon) or the Wild East (New York), from the Deep South (Georgia) or the deep North (Michigan), are prepared to call themselves 'Americans'.[1]

1. There are, of course, no such people as 'the British', either. A man is either an Englishman, or a Scotsman, or a Welshman, or an Irishman; only newly naturalized people would describe themselves as British; and the Americans talk of the British.

There is a legend (which plenty of songs and poems try
to keep alive) that America does something peculiar to
your soul. Well, it certainly does; but it does not transform a Central European bank-clerk, a Negro jazz
musician, a Syrian bookmaker, a Japanese wrestler, a
Sicilian tourist-guide or a Scandinavian sailor, in no
time, into that instantly recognizable, wonderful and
unique paragon of humanity, the *Homo Americanus,* as
they are so fond of maintaining. The Swiss know
better than to make such a claim. It is not only that the
Swiss French will have nothing to do with the Swiss
Germans while neither of them will have anything to do
with the Swiss Italians — life is never quite as simple as
that. Ask a man from Lausanne what he thinks of the people of Geneva; ask the same man of Lausanne if he likes
the people of Berne; ask a man of Basle if he would like
to be taken for a man from Zürich; ask a man of Chur,
in eastern Switzerland, if he feels himself nearer to the
man in the moon or to a man from St Gallen. There is a
saying that there are three qualifications any Bishop of
Chur should possess: (1) he must be a Roman Catholic;
(2) he must be a consecrated priest; and (3) he must be a
native of Chur or, at least, of the Canton of Graubünden.
But — people like to add — the first two requirements
might be dispensed with.

I once knew a charming old gentleman, a prominent
manufacturer in one of the three original Cantons, who
had classified all his compatriots very precisely. He
would never employ a man from Appenzell (forty-
three miles north-east from his village), because people
from Appenzell are 'impertinent and mean'; people
coming from about twenty-five miles south of Appenzell
— the people of Grisons or Graubünden — while quite
different were not much better, because though they
were certainly capable they were utterly unreliable;
people from about thirteen miles to the north of Appen-

zell — the people of St Gallen — were quite different again, in fact people from another planet, but they were of no use at all because they were a lazy lot; people of Berne were too slow-witted, and people from Lucerne too weak and irremediably spoilt by the tourists. In short — no people were any good at all, except those from his immediate neighbourhood who, however, were all rotters anyway, and not to be touched with a barge pole. When his son — who was also his general manager — married, he moved out of the paternal home and went to live with his wife in Zug, about twelve miles away (but in another Canton), from whence he drove daily to his job in his father's factory. After eighteen months, his father managed not only to quarrel with him but also to drive him out of his job. The son is convinced that the real reason for this break was his father's deep and unalterable conviction that the 'people of Zug are petty and calculating'.

In the early nineteenth century the inhabitants of the small village of Ernen refused the use of their gallows for the execution of a convicted murderer, a resident of the neighbouring village. 'Sorry,' they said, 'these gallows are for us and for our children.'

This ethnic variety, these irreconcilable differences between the people of Appenzell and those of Schwyz (divided from each other by forty-three infinite miles), between the people of Zug and those of Winterthur, make Switzerland one of the biggest countries in the world. This mutual dislike, contempt and healthy detestation of one another is the firm foundation of Swiss democracy and neutrality. 'Love thy neighbour' says the Christian teaching — and a profound and noble teaching it certainly is. But loving Christians fought each other for thirty years in a devastating and cruel war in the seventeenth century and, indeed, during long centuries before and ever since. No — you cannot love someone if you simply detest him. Ask any man of Basle if he could possibly love a man of Zürich, ask a man of Olten if he could possibly love a man of Aarau. You cannot love him but you can *tolerate* him. And love, if not sincere is hypocrisy; but *tolerance* is the shining democratic virtue. For the people of Basle to tolerate the people of Zürich as neighbours is an incredible act of self-discipline; for the people of Uri to live in peaceful co-existence with that impertinent and mean lot at Appenzell is a great and admirable achievement; for the people of Lausanne to restrain themselves and start no wars of revenge against the Bernese, who once invaded and subjugated them, is the pinnacle of civilized self-control. I knew a lady in Schaffhausen, on the Rhine, whose son married a girl from Winterthur — about fifteen miles away. She was heartbroken, of course, and explained to me in great confidence that she was making a great effort to treat her daughter-in-law 'as if she were one of us' although she knew very well that these 'mixed marriages never worked'. She, too, regarded herself as a miracle of self-sacrifice and of almost superhuman control.

And that is the whole point. The human soul needs to get rid of a certain amount of hatred and nastiness just as an internal combustion engine must get rid of a certain amount of poisonous gas. The Swiss get rid of these gases by despising each other so intensely that they have no energy to spare for hating the rest of humanity. Look at Germany, to mention only one example: since her unification she has plunged the world into two world wars. It seems to be clear that the original unification of Germany was bad luck for humanity. And humanity hardly knows how lucky it is that there is no hope, not the faintest chance whatsoever of bringing about the unification of Switzerland.

Just Luck

I have an extremely talented relative who is something of a mathematical genius and, on top of it, one of the most modest persons I know. He has never regarded any achievement of his as really his: it was 'just luck'. In fact, there was a time when I used to address him as 'Just Luck'. It was just luck when at the age of twenty he was offered so many scholarships at Princeton University that he had to decline some: it was simply not worth while taking them because his income tax would have run too high. It was also just luck when, at the age of twenty-one, during the war, he was sent to Los Alamos to work on the atomic bomb. He had good luck again when he was appointed assistant to Albert Einstein; it was just luck when he became a full professor at Princeton University in his late twenties, and he had further luck when, just under thirty, he became head of the mathematical department of one of the Ivy League universities and eventually its President. It was just luck, he said earnestly, and I believe he meant it.

I am reminded of this attitude when I hear people say that Switzerland is so lucky to possess all that natural beauty. To some extent she certainly is: no amount of human endeavour and devotion could make Saudi Arabia half as beautiful. But a great deal of Switzerland is man-made beauty. They make the best of nature's gifts. Austria and Yugoslavia could be just as beautiful: all nature's gifts are there. For some people, indeed, Switzerland is too elaborate and a minority prefer Austria or Yugoslavia, on the grounds that their beauty is more natural and unspoilt. But this 'elaboration' is not luck: it is the result of a lot of work. Switzerland may be 'spoilt' for some; but all that 'spoiling' is the result of hard work. It may be ridiculous to find an hotel on every mountain top and 'Pass Höhe' but it is not 'just luck' that the hotels are there. They were built there. It may be amusing to see innumerable ski-lifts, chair-lifts and funiculars all over the place, but ski-lifts and the rest do not grow like fir-trees: they have to be produced by certain artificial methods.

The Swiss, indeed, are hard-working people and this devotion to work is one of their most repulsive virtues. Altogether, it is the virtues of the Swiss which I find a

bit hard to bear. Coming from England, I regard work as some sort of nuisance you must pretend to be engaged in between cups of tea. But the Swiss take work seriously: they start early, finish late, and are even proud of it. They are paid for it handsomely — more handsomely than the English — and their old-fashioned idea is that

they ought to play fair. The employer is not simply the
chap you organize strikes against: he must pay, to be
sure, and pay a lot, but he must also receive value for
his money. This attitude is, of course, quite outmoded
in the last third of the twentieth century.

Another Swiss virtue that tends to drive me slightly
crazy is their kindness and politeness. I am speaking now
of German Switzerland only. Whatever is going on — in
an office, in a shop, in a restaurant, in all fields of
private life — they keep on saying *'Bitte schön'* almost
endlessly, to which you are supposed to reply *'Danke
schön'*. Should you stop this exchange of *'Bitte schön-
Danke schön'* before twenty-two rounds are up (and with
a few exclamations of *'Ja gerne'* thrown in), you are
regarded as a barbarian. I have seen people drop with
exhaustion and their last words before passing out completely were a few whispered *'Danke schöns'* or *'Bitte
schöns'*. You have to say *'Grütsi'* to all and sundry all
the time. This is a Swiss greeting and you cannot say it
often enough. You do not really say it, you sing it.
When you meet several people, you say, *'Grütsi miten-
ander . . . '* or something like that and it sounds like a
whole operatic aria from the mouth of any true-born
Swiss. In wild mountain passes, everyone you meet will
sing *'Grütsi'* to you. You sing *'Grütsi'* to them and exchange, if you have any manners at all, a few *'Danke
schöns'* and *'Bitte schöns'*. You'll be quite hoarse by the
time you part. Once, near Interlaken, I was walking
alone in the mountains of the Bernese Oberland when I
saw a solitary cow coming towards me. She stopped. I
stepped out of her way but she did not move. She went
on looking at me with her sad brown eyes. There we
were, the cow and I, neither of us would move. I was
nonplussed. At last, after two or three minutes, I said,
'Grütsi'. She nodded to me seriously and walked on.

The honesty of the Swiss is not easy to bear either. I

do not insist on being diddled as one is diddled fifty times a day in Venice or Naples. I can do without that reasonably well. I do not mind if in restaurants I know that there is no need to check the bill because it is unlikely that the waitress has added in the date. But there comes a point when you feel that honesty has gone a little too far: when everybody's honesty is always in his buttonhole. Too much shining honesty tends to blind you a little. A year or two ago my wife and I went into a shop that had a number of electric irons displayed in the window, to see if we could leave a few things to be cleaned and ironed. It turned out, however, that the shop was not a cleaner's but a place where they sold electric irons. 'Sorry,' we said and turned to leave. The lady behind the counter, unwilling to see us disappointed, offered to lend us an iron for a day or two. My wife accepted gladly: how much was the rent? Oh nothing, the lady said, there was no charge. My wife then offered to leave a deposit which the lady refused. My wife then wanted to leave our name and address at least — upon which I dragged her out of the shop and fled. I realized that the shopkeeper lady was getting suspicious and had started looking at us as if we were habitual criminals: the ideas we had! The fact that we were offering deposits and trying to leave our name and address clearly proved that we were the kind of people to whom the *possibility* had occurred that an electric iron might be stolen. This was suspicious indeed. I took to my heels because I was afraid she might call the police.

But the most terrifying and off-putting of all Swiss virtues is cleanliness. I personally am not enamoured of cleanliness. It is a Germanic virtue and I am all for a little Latin dirt. Not too much of it — one can go too far — but a little surely lends colour to life. But when you go on making jokes for years about the Swiss hoovering their roads between villages and then, one day, you actually *see* a vast electric hoover cleaning the open road, then you say to yourself that this mania for cleanliness has got out of hand. When you realize that a roadsweeper and a dustman are actually cleaner in Switzerland than many a waiter in certain other countries, then you start longing for just a little dirt here and there.

This problem has, however, its glorious side, too. The Swiss have, in fact, solved the perennial question which has troubled philosophers throughout the centuries: What is the aim of life? The answer the Swiss give to this question is simple, original, and convincing: The aim of life is to make your door-handle shine.

The Glory of Krins

In February, 1971, Swiss women ceased to be the laughing stock of Western Europe: they obtained the right to vote. At last they have become equal, although men still remain considerably more equal than women. One cannot help asking the question: why did it take so long? Why was Switzerland, this ancient democracy, so late in giving her women the rights which other women possessed not only in other democracies but also under several quite tyrannical forms of government?

The usual answer to this question has been: the Swiss are no more reactionary than other people, only slower. On reflection this reply cannot stand. First of all, the Swiss are extremely fast, eager and up-to-date in all technical matters and business administration. When it comes to automation, computerisation and such, the Swiss are the Americans of Europe. Yet they are exasperatingly slow when it comes to the changing of social habits, their way of life, their traditions, their values.

I have just gone through the notes I made for this chapter and I see that seven of the nine women I interviewed remarked: 'This is the land of the male chauvinist pig.' This *cri de coeur*, however, simply means that the Swiss are like the rest of us.

We are all male chauvinist pigs, except for women who are female chauvinist pigs. The human psyche works in such a way that we all (well, deduct a tiny percentage for the exceptions who make the rule valid) are keen on establishing the fact that we — whoever we may be —

are the finest specimen of humanity. Whether we are
English, French, Chinese or Bulgarian, we believe that
we are tops — although we may well allow that the other,
minor, races should be treated with condescending tolerance. Now, if all the non-Schwitzerdeutsch-speaking part
of humanity is put into an inferior category, this simple
move establishes the superiority of quite a lot of
people — it elevates them to a sort of plateau. But they

would rather be on a *pinnacle* than a plateau, and they
can halve the number of their rivals if, given that they
are male, they treat women as their inferiors. Like everyone else, the Swiss male then becomes incomparably
better than (1) people of other countries; (2) if he lives
in a town, people from other towns or who live in the
country; (3) if he lives in the country, people who live
in a town; (4) people who live in a different part of his
town (our own address is always just right, neither
'snobbish' nor 'slummy'); (5) people with a different
profession; (6) people who have a different hobby (our
own hobby, whether reading, riding, studying geology,
fox-hunting, working for the comfort of flat-footed
dogs, breeding hamsters or playing tiddlywinks is always
more natural, more noble, more intellectual than anyone
else's); (7) people who belong to a different family (the

sad fact that we aren't on speaking terms with a single member of our own family never has anything to do with its undoubted superiority); and (8) people of the opposite sex. Well, if we belong to the finest nation, live in its best place, practice the best profession, indulge in the most admirable hobbies, belong to the most distinguished family, and to the better sex — what follows from that?

It is the pleasing inference which has to be drawn from the above which makes people a little slow in changing their attitudes. Most of the English, for example, still rule the vastest Empire the world has ever known and are loyal subjects of their ageing Queen, Victoria; in France General de Gaulle still rules the land; in the United States the dollar is still, for many millions, as almighty as it was a quarter of a century ago. The Swiss are more modest: they stick only to the idea of male superiority. They have not really been slower than the rest of us: they have simply preferred that comparatively harmless way of being better.

The Swiss version of the de Gaulle complex is the Krins-complex. De Gaulle, with breath-taking arrogance and self-confidence, was always ready to believe that he was right and the rest of the world was out of step. If he wasn't *quite* right, that did not matter: he felt only the deepest contempt for the rest of the world in any case. De Gaulle is no longer with us; the village of Krins still is.

Swiss women received the *federal* vote first; then the cantonal vote and, finally, the vote in their own communes. But not *all* communes (and not even all half-cantons as yet). The village of Krins — a Catholic village in a Protestant area — is one of the last-ditchers. Women in the village of Krins are still denied the vote. Or rather they have a say as to which Party should rule Switzerland, but not as to whether a right of way should be established in Krins. I do not share the views of the villagers of Krins when it comes to women's emancipation; but I raise my hat to their stubbornness, their Gaullish arrogance and bloody-mindedness – characteristics I always envy in others but completely lack myself.

The fight for the freedom of Swiss women is on. It is well organised, intelligent, purposeful; it is also non-militant and rather tepid. They make the usual demands for civic rights, equal pay, abortions etc. They think that a woman should be the President of Switzerland one day, but not yet. That women should be members of the government one day, but not yet. That girls should be allowed in grammar schools — which now they are: it is one, and only one, of their successes. Equality may be reached in two ways: women may become government ministers or men may become nannies. Why are certain professions — Swiss women ask — left entirely to women? This is as insulting as being completely excluded from some others. Why are there not, for example, male kindergarten teachers? Children need a father-substitute as much as they need a mother-substitute, declare Pestalozzi's descendants. The 'Men to the Kindergarten' movement is another of their successes. There *are* men in the kindergarten now, looking after toddlers. This is the sensible Swiss equivalent of burning bras.

One of the obstacles to women's emancipation is that a considerable number of women refuse to be emancipated. In Switzerland these ladies are referred to as the 'Green Windows' because they live in the garden belts, take no interest in politics and other public affairs and spend their time looking out of their green windows, watching the trivial events of the street with breathless excitement. These women are the worst enemies of

Women's Lib and I am its most enthusiastic supporter. First of all, I have always seen the justice of the women's case. Then, I am ready to go further than any Germaine Greer. I am not only prepared to accept women as our equals but as our superiors. They should have *all* the jobs they want, provided one of them keeps me in com-

fort — indeed, in luxury. While she goes out to work, I am quite prepared to cook for her, clean the house or just keep an eye on the maids — or perhaps the lads. With a little bit of luck I shall be allowed to do some writing; if not, I shall spend my time looking out of the Green Window. My lady and mistress can buy me as much jewellery as she wishes, but let it be known that I do not care for furs. I hope she will frequently return home with a nice bunch of flowers. I promise I shall not rebel against my fate. I do not want to be emancipated, and considering the general level of politics, I do not even want the vote.

Democracy with a Schwitzerdeutsch Accent

If it is not easy to forgive the virtues of the Swiss, they do luckily possess some redeeming sins which endear them to all of us.

The first case to mention is the Swiss version of democracy, which is democracy with a strong Schwitzerdeutsch accent. The Constitution in its original form was evolved from the pact of 1291.

The Swiss, while passionately interested in other people's politics, do not get over-excited about their own. They are great newspaper readers and their small country has some of the greatest newspapers in the world; also some of the dullest. In some cases these two characteristics go together. The *Neue Zürcher Zeitung,* for example, would be not only a most reputable and highbrow paper, but quite a readable one if only it were readable — I mean acceptable to the eye, instead of being a hopelessly old-fashioned black sea of practically indistinguishable small letters.

The Swiss can become passionately interested in revolutions in Venezuela, Chinese threats to Nepal, party splits in Zaìre, and economic crises in Cuba, but they are not unduly agitated about goings-on in Berne. They feel a little parochial and are shy about their own affairs; they always speak of their own politics with an apologetic smile, as a matter of no importance — i.e. of no international consequence. They seem to be a little ashamed that they never give the world any trouble; that they behave like more or less normal human beings and

practically never threaten to plunge Europe into war, as
any other small nation with a modicum of self-respect
does at least twice a decade. They are fully aware that a
debate about a new federal tax cannot possibly be so
absorbing and exciting as a political hijacking in Rome;
and when that new tax is abolished after a few years,
that again is not half so dramatic as the opening of a
new chapter in the Arab-Israeli war.

Swiss democracy has developed into something like a
part-time job for the citizen. The Swiss Constitution is a
federal one, like the American: each Canton is, in fact,
a little republic in full control of its internal affairs,
such as education, public health, police, cantonal taxes,
etc. On top of it, there are federal problems and numer-
ous municipal questions. The democratically minded
Swiss have developed two special and attractive institutions: the referendum and the right of initiative. Private
citizens (under conditions laid down in the Constitution)
are entitled to initiate legislation; and the Federal
Government can quite easily be forced to submit certain
measures to referendum and, in fact, in many cases does
so without any coercion at all. It is easy to see where all
this overdose of democracy leads: it means that the
Swiss are kept pretty busy rushing to the ballot box.
They have to voice their opinions (via the ballot box)
on federal, cantonal and municipal laws, policies and
enactments, without respite.

A few years ago a friend of mine remarked that the
glory of Switzerland was that no one knew who her
President was. Most of us have heard the name of Richard
Nixon; few of us know that a gentleman called Dr. Nello
Celio (one of Nixon's Swiss contemporaries) exists.
Indeed, no people outside Switzerland have heard of
him; and few inside.

Switzerland is the democracy where election results
do not really matter. The Swiss Parliament has two

chambers, the National Council (with 200 members) and a Council of State, a body similar in its composition to the United States Senate (with 44 members). The two chambers together form the Federal Assembly. This Assembly has wide powers — first of all legislative. It also elects, every year, the President and the Vice Presi-

dent from among members of the government. If you are a member of the government you are pretty sure that your turn will come sooner or later to be President, but it is obvious, this type of election is not over-dramatic. The Federal Assembly also elects from among its members the government, called the Federal Council. The government has seven members and the President and the Vice-President also hold portfolios. Members of the government belong to various parties — and the balance in this coalition has been worked out carefully, after long strife. So no one is keen on changing this balance of power inside the government and, unless there is a landslide victory for one party or another (unlikely in the foreseeable future) the composition of the government will remain unchanged for a long time. It is in this sense that election results do not really matter in Switzerland. What excitement Swiss democracy can generate, does not reach the public. Most of the controversial issues are settled in Committees. Quite a few young people are dissatisfied with this method. They want real rights, not just the right to say yes or no.

One experienced Swiss politician shrugged his shoulders when I put this to him.

'Even to say *yes* or *no* is often dangerous enough. To say *no* may be disastrous although one would not dream of saying *yes*.'

Perhaps. This sounds very much like the questionable wisdom of an old fox. But he added something more convincing:

'We Swiss have the habit of approving large projects but when credit is needed, we refuse the cash. We want, say, a brand new airport as long as it does not cost any money.'

Everything is calm, quiet and efficient. Everything is beautifully dull, too. I really mean *beautifully*. After all, the job of a government is not to supply entertainment for foreign newspaper readers but to govern the country efficiently. This the Swiss Federal Council does. And God save Switzerland and the world from the day when we all learn the Swiss President's name.

Militarism

The Swiss, contrary to general belief, are one of the most militaristic nations of Europe. In the United States and even in the Soviet Union a smaller and smaller percentage of the population has to serve in the armed forces. In Switzerland there is no question of a percentage: in Switzerland everybody is a soldier. In September 1939 all the Swiss passes were fully manned even before Britain declared war on Germany and today there is no country in Europe where one sees so many soldiers practising sharp-shooting and mountain climbing, or engaged in other military exercises, as in Switzerland. If a nation wants to fight it need not be very powerful: it is enough to have powerful allies. But if you are determined to stay out of it all and not to fight, then you must be really strong.

All Swiss men are in the reserve and have to keep their uniform, full kit, and their guns at home, ready for any emergency. When the Swiss *Hausfrau* has finished polishing the door-handles, she gets out her husband's gun and gives it a good polish, too. As time goes by, weapons become more sophisticated and one would think that this domestic idyll of guns becomes slightly outdated. Not at all. People nowadays take home submachine guns and automatic rifles and their wives polish them up as efficiently as they did the simple or domestic rifle. Some people drive home in armoured cars and these are occasionally parked in the courtyards of farms. Polaris missiles have not yet appeared on the scene, mostly because the Swiss stick to defensive weapons. Polaris' missiles may or may not come in the future. Some potential aggressor may be caught unawares. But not the Swiss *Hausfrau*: she is ready with her rag and polish. There are innumerable jokes about these guns in the larder but the point surely is that a government must trust its citizens if it can afford to keep them armed all the time. Can anyone imagine what would happen if

all the citizens in, say, Czechoslovakia, were given guns? It is far from certain that they would all be used according to government instructions. But an outbreak of revolution in Switzerland is about as likely as an outbreak of democracy in Russia or a heatwave in Greenland.

Once a soldier, always a soldier. In Switzerland they simply will not let you go. There are various types of services you have to perform according to your age. People over ninety are put on slightly lighter duties — that is all.

On Money

A lot of people say they do not like the Swiss because they love money too much. Money has certainly become very popular with many people recently, and not only the Swiss. The sixties were the classical era of the businessman; money took the centre of the stage and even sex and crime were forced to play second and third fiddle. I do not think that this did much to change the attitude of the Swiss towards money. They have always loved it but they do not love it now any more than before. It is largely a question of what sort of money you love. The Swiss franc is a kind worth loving.

But do the Swiss really *love* money? I do not think so. It would be more exact to say they *revere* it. They have a high respect for it.

To throw money about with careless, grand-seigneurish abandon is certainly not one of the more conspicuous Swiss characteristics. A few years ago I wrote a short story about a Hungarian baron who squandered two fortunes on smashing mirrors, tables, chairs, and other furniture in pubs. It was his idea of a good time. I do not say that his was a particularly intelligent or commendable pastime but it was nothing special in pre-war Hungary; it was not even remarkable. But any Swiss man worthy of his nationality would much rather die than smash one single glass deliberately, if he would have to pay for it afterwards.

There are few Swiss millionaires; but there are even fewer Swiss paupers. Their wealth is solid, traditional and inherited, even if each of them adds his mite to the family fortune. You can meet some of those rare Swiss millionaires travelling second class because 'second is just as good as first'; and in Berne you can find the President of the Swiss Republic in the tram queue, going to his office at a quarter to eight so as not to be late.

I have a Swiss friend whom I have always regarded as rather un-Swiss: he is broad-minded, cosmopolitan, and very easy-going, indeed generous with his money. I have stayed in his house on several occasions and his hospitality was not only warm — as is usual in Switzerland — but lavish. So I was really astonished to find, when he came to stay with me in England, that he was prepared to devote four or five days to the problems of buying a raincoat. He visited two dozen shops, returned to one many times, tried the same coat on twice a day — once in the morning and once in the afternoon — and then sped to other shops to see if he could not get a better coat cheaper. When at home, at our place, he spent half of his time switching off the light in rooms where we had carelessly left it on. I decided in the end that all Swiss were alike after all and that there were no exceptions. So I was really surprised a year later when I visited him once again in Switzerland and found out something extraordinary about him. We took the funicular in his village. There were three of us — my wife, my friend, and I — but he bought only two tickets. I said nothing, but noticing that I was somewhat perplexed he explained, 'I don't need a ticket.'

'Why?'

'I just don't,' he replied somewhat curtly and mysteriously.

In the evening he explained. His village had had no funicular and this had offended his local pride. Why should his village be a miserable exception? It had to have a funicular — so he had one built at his own expense which he presented to the municipality. His only condition was that he and his family were to be allowed to use it without payment to the end of time.

'Well, you deserve that much honour at least . . . '

'Honour? Who wants honour?' he retorted. 'I want to save on the fare.'

Still, I did not find this explanation quite satisfactory and I returned to the attack next day. I asked him quite openly how could a man capable of such generosity towards his village, be as petty as he was about a raincoat?

'You don't understand,' he said. 'I wanted my village to have a funicular, and a funicular costs money. Heaps of money — so I had to pay heaps. But to buy a poor raincoat when you can get a better one is waste. And waste is just stupid. For example, to illuminate your flat as if it were a fun-fair is a reasonable luxury; if you like strong lights, do so by all means. But to leave lights on in an unoccupied room is waste. It is sin.'

Years later I met him by chance in a restaurant in Zürich. He asked me to sit down at his table. He was having some antipasta which he invited me to sample. When I declined he insisted. Finally, I gave in: and indeed I had never tasted anything quite so good. So I went on tasting it. During our subsequent conversation he told me he had had a museum built in his village, too, and endowed it with several famous paintings.

'It must have cost as much as the funicular,' I remarked.

'More,' he replied drily, then asked for the bill and left.

When I rose to leave later, I noticed that the price of half an antipasta had been put on my bill. Well, I had tasted it.

This surprised me a little. But it should not have done so. And I shall certainly remember the Swiss film-magnate who took me to a coffee-house to discuss some business involving tens of thousands of francs and then paid for his own coffee and let me pay for mine. The idea was that the tens of thousands were to be fees, fully deserved by me; but why should he *give me* — just like that — two francs?

But the gold medal for pettiness goes to another Swiss. Last year I met an English girl — an old acquaintance of mine from London — in Geneva, who told me in tears that she had been defrauded by a Swiss gentleman. This sounded unlikely. And, indeed, next day the Swiss man in question alleged that in fact it was she who had tried to cheat *him*. It turned out that this English girl had settled in Geneva and was earning her living as a translator. Translation is paid per thousand words. As a newcomer to Switzerland, she did what she had always done in England: she *estimated* the number of words and made it out to the nearest thousand.

'She charged me for 8,000 words,' the outraged Swiss complained, 'instead of 7,839: that is to say, 200 francs instead of 197 francs 15 centimes.'

'But how do you know it was 7,839 words?' I asked incredulously. 'You don't mean to say you counted them? Each word?'

'Of course I counted them. And my secretary verified it. It was 7,839 all right.'

I took the work home and counted the words myself. There were, in fact, 7,887 words — forty-eight more than he and his secretary had made it. I told him about this when we met the next morning. But he was even more outraged than before.

'Oh no,' he exclaimed. 'Surely not. There were forty-eight *proper nouns* in the text. You do not expect me to pay hard cash for the alleged translation of names of people or towns?'

'I certainly do,' I replied. 'In some cases these names are different. Horatius is Horace in English; Vergilius is Virgil; München is Munich, and Wien is Vienna. These words surely ought to count. They have to be translated.'

He was upset because he did not want to be unfair. Mean, yes; unfair, no. It took him a whole day to work out a compromise. In future — he said the next day — he would pay half-rate for all truly translated proper nouns (for 'Wien' but not for 'London'), i.e. roughly one and a quarter centimes instead of two and a half.

I faithfully communicated this compromise to the translator. She listened carefully and then reflected for some three or four minutes. Then she packed her bag and returned to live in England.

The Gnomes of Zürich

The state religion of Switzerland is Banking. The official religion of the City of London is also Banking. In Britain we have the following religious holidays: Easter, Whitsun, Christmas and Bank Holiday. In other countries Banking remains an important but secular activity. In Switzerland there are more banks than dentists and consequently people's financial life is healthier than their teeth.

Whenever Swiss banking interests clash with those of the City, the conflict takes on the appearance and

intensity of mediaeval, religious feuds about some dogma. The Banking War, of course, with its sequences of Battles of the Sterling, has serious economic consequences. There is nothing new in this. After all, the Thirty Years War ravaged large parts of Europe and the Crusades large parts of the Middle East. Religion and good-will have always been more destructive than down-right savagery.

The zealots — in all religious wars — call their adver-saries nasty names, thus the phrase *Gnomes of Zürich* was born. The so-called heretics, on their part, regard themselves as true believers and upholders of ortho-doxy. The Gnomes of Zürich refuse to blush and I am on their side.

Swiss bankers are not my favourite people. Not that other bankers are. Not that I am *their* favourite. Once in Zürich I saw a man (in the city's last famous coffee-house, not in existence any more) studying something that looked from the distance like a magazine. The man looked not only respectable but the very incarnation of respectability: dark suit, square haircut, rimless spec-tacles — the lot. Yet his face grew lewd and lecherous as he chuckled over his reading material — it was obvious-ly obscene. I stood up, walked slowly by his table and threw a glance at his reading. It was a balance sheet. First I felt taken aback, almost outraged. Soon my contempt turned into envy. This man had a pleasure in life I shall never experience. I shall never read (let alone enjoy) a truly titillating balance sheet.

It is, of course, absurd to blame the so-called Gnomes of Zürich for our troubles. Speculation hardly ever causes weakness; weakness of a currency causes specula-tion. But the Gnomes of Zürich are no speculators, they are respectable international bankers. They are tough businessmen whose loyalties belong to their client and not to Mr Harold Wilson's Labour Government. (It was Mr Wilson, who made the phrase *Gnomes of Zürich* notorious.) Their conception of duty is to see to it that their clients' money is safe and not that Mr Wilson should stay in office. Whenever the pound has become weak, they have moved into deutschmark or dollar. But it has not only been the Swiss bankers who did this:

British businessmen — legal or illegal holders of foreign currencies — have done the same. The Gnomes of London did it and do it; the Gnomes of Birmingham do it; the Gnomes of Manchester do it. The Gnomes can hardly be expected to tell their clients: 'Yes, if you stick to pound sterling, you stand to lose about 20-25 per cent of your money; but it is your duty to the international community to stick to it and never mind the loss!' It is not the sort of advice to which clients take kindly.

If I have one quarrel with the Gnomes of Zürich it is that they fail to acknowledge that they are interested in their clients' money alone. They are hypocrites, like the rest of us, and keep talking about their concern for the community and their international duties; morality is on their lips as often as if they were archbishops. The welfare of the community means the community of

their investors; humanity means that part of humanity which entrusts its money to them. Their love for humanity is great; but their interpretation of humanity is narrow.

I have discussed the reasons for Britain's economic plight with many a Gnome and with other economists. Their views are not the subject of the present treatise. Quite a few of them, however, were intrigued by the idea of a British Army on the Rhine. They regarded it as a ludicrous anachronism at this time. A German

Army on the Thames, they think, would be more appropriate and incomparably more profitable for Britain. And what about a Swiss contingent; the President's Own Gnomes thrown in? But this would be a sane move and sanity always seemed absurd.

They also blame — as you would expect them to do — the Trade Unions and the Labour Party for our economic ills. They kept talking of the Gnomes of Transport House which personally I thought a little tiresome.

On Invasion and the Freedom to Detest One Another

Switzerland suffered no foreign invasion between the time of Napoleon and the middle nineteen-fifties. The Napoleonic invasion was given short shrift: with the help of their allies and their own staunch resistance, the Swiss dealt with that threat. But that was an easy problem. Napoleon and his army tried to conquer them only with guns and swords; the new invaders, German businessmen, use money. And the Swiss have always found it much easier to resist bullets than to resist cash.

In the last few years the Germans, who have always been passionately devoted to the south and the sun, invaded Ticino (the Italian-speaking Canton) to such an extent that the people became seriously worried. A great deal of the land was being bought up, modern and functional villas of exceptional ugliness were being built; German as a language almost replaced Italian and soon there will be standing room only in the Ticino. Watching the Gotthard Tunnel at Easter — the endless queues of German cars waiting to be taken across — one has the impression of being in Bavaria. The Germans, of course, bring a lot of money with them and spread prosperity, and there is nothing wrong with them. Nevertheless some Swiss, mostly those not in a position to profit from the soaring price of real estate, have blamed the people of Ticino for selling out to the Germans. Many others, quite genuinely and without any ulterior motive, disliked the idea that the Germans, having lost the Cameroons, should set about colonizing southern Switzerland instead.

There is an invasion of American businessmen, too: they prefer to have their European head offices in Switzerland, because money is freely transferable and the policy of Swiss neutrality also has a soothing effect on their nerves. Besides, you can always make a bargain with the tax authorities.

But the real troubles in Switzerland are always domestic, and the only invasion of consequence is also an internal one. Switzerland being a tri-lingual country, it would seem to be the duty of any good Swiss to pick up all three federal languages. But there is one-way traffic only. The French-speaking Swiss never learn German; while Schwitzerdeutsch they regard as a barbaric dialect. Those whose mother tongue is Italian learn neither French nor German unless, of course, they happen to get a job in a French or German-speaking area and they have to. It is the industrious German-speaking Swiss who travel to the French parts in great numbers and learn French. Your French-Swiss friends, when they meet a waitress or a shop assistant with a heavy German accent, will sigh with disgust and exchange sad, ferocious looks: 'The enemy within the walls . . . '

The Swiss covet no territory from any other country and no Swiss territory has secessionist ideas. Their surplus energy is used up internally. The only secessionist movement boiling up is in the Canton of Berne, which is the largest Canton and is, of course, German speaking. But it has an enclave of French-speakers who wish to secede and form a new Canton, to be called Jura. (This is, by the way, *'merci vielmals'* country, so proud of its pure Gallic tongue.) Demonstrations take place, speeches are made, and slogans of *'Jura Libre!'* are painted on the walls. The rebel-complex is as strong in some people as the inferiority-complex or the Oedipuscomplex is in others: yet these poor, heroic souls have no better cause than to rebel against the vile oppression of Canton Berne.

Separatism in the Jura district flared up before the First World War but, naturally enough, died down during the war itself. It exploded once again in 1947 when the French-speaking population suffered what it regarded as a grave linguistic insult. The *Comité de Moutier* was then formed and political agitation led to a plebiscite in July 1959, when the cause of separatism suffered a defeat. The defeat, however — the separatists maintain — does not count. The whole Canton voted for continued unity; but the three French-speaking districts (Delsberg, Pruntrut and Freiberge) voted overwhelmingly for separation. The will of the people must prevail — all agree on that; but views differ as to who the people are. (The obvious parallel is a possible plebiscite on Irish Unity. Who should vote: the Northern Irish? *All* the Irish? The entire United Kingdom? Such a procedural decision might be more decisive than the actual plebiscite itself.)

After the plebiscite of 1959 the issue has remained alive. Sporadic unrest continues. There were noisy separatist demonstrations in Berne in January 1967; there was an invasion of the sacred chambers of the Federal Assembly during a presidential election in December 1968; the Swiss army in the Jura was labelled an army of occupation, and even a few bombs exploded in the Canton itself. The fight is still on. It is regarded as unpleasant, outrageous and violent in Switzerland; it would be regarded as a peaceful idyll in Belfast.

A Bernese cantonal official told me: 'We are going to suppress the movement.'

'How?' I asked him with keen interest. 'Are you going to open fire? Call in the troops?'

'Of course not. There are more subtle and much more effective methods. I shall explain to them what independent cantonal administration *costs*. I assure you, what with police, roads, schools, administrative buildings and many other items it comes to a pretty penny. That will cool their secessionist fever.' (In fact, a local plebiscite has now decided in favour of separation. A national referendum is to follow, but *Jura Libre* is a step nearer.)

The international peace and wise tolerance of the Swiss nation is based, as I have already said, on a healthy mutual detestation of each other. This is really the main clue to the wisdom of the Swiss. If 'Love thy neighbour as thyself' is the first Christian duty of any true-born Swiss, 'Hate thy neighbour more than thyself' is the second. Niedwalden and Obwalden are the smallest Cantons (really sub-Cantons only) in Switzerland, but the fact that Niedwalden fought against Napoleon more than a century and a half ago, while Obwalden did not, is still the source of undying enmity between the two races (the races of Niedwalden and Obwalden, I mean). A Niedwalden man told me once:

'Intermarriage is quite out of the question. I would rather give my daughter to a man of Winterthur than to someone from Obwalden.'

'Rather to a man of Winterthur. . . !' Strong words.

Or take Basle just once again. They regard themselves, and with some justification, as more French than Swiss; and even more German than Swiss: after all, the Rhine is their river. People from Basle hop over to Alsace for supper and for a business conference to Germany; crossing the frontier means no more to them than crossing the street does to us.

'There is no prostitution in Basle,' a Basler friend once told me. 'Not because we are so virtuous. But, you see, we hop over much too often. . . . '

In spite of this valuable piece of information, I could not help noticing in the streets of Basle that my informant was not quite truthful, and I said so the next

day. He grinned. 'Oh, we must have a few girls . . . .
They are for the sake of visiting Zürich businessmen. . . .'

When he noticed my somewhat astonished face, he added in haste: 'I don't want you to misunderstand me. I do not hate the Zürchers . . . I only despise them.'

Love Thy Scapegoat

There has been one other invasion which has caused the Swiss a lot of headaches: the invasion of the *gastarbeiter* or guest workers, a modern version of indentured labour under a euphemistic name. The problem in a nutshell, as it is often summed up in Switzerland, is this: the Swiss meant to import cheap labour and they found that they had imported human beings.

The problem, of course, is not unique to Switzerland and when other nations preach to the Swiss, it is a case of the kettle calling the pot black. Such denigration of the pot by the kettle may lack a sound moral basis but it is not bad in practice: pot and kettle should remind each other that both are black. Mutual abuse is not such a bad form of education.

While the problem of guestworkers (or coloured immigrants) exists elsewhere it is specially acute in Switzerland. It does make a difference whether a million strangers are absorbed by, say, 50 million or just by 6 million natives.

The Swiss jingoes declare that there are not enough Swiss about. Perhaps they are right. I have said earlier that the Swiss get along with their neighbours (and the rest of humanity) so well because the human soul needs to get rid of a certain amount of nastiness and the Swiss could get rid of these poisonous gases by despising one another. But there are not enough Swiss; so they need the *gastarbeiter* too.

All nations seem to need Jews. Some speak of 'out-groups' and others use other names, but 'Jews' is a convenient term. I intend it to mean those we use to give us the feeling of superiority which every human being and group is striving for, usually in vain. There are two main methods of achieving this illusion. The more difficult one is just to be superior; the other is to create inferior groups or to call other groups inferior. It is — in Trade Union parlance — the 'differentials' that count. Now, the Jews used to be excellent material for being Jews, but not any more. After Hitler new Jews had to be found to serve the purpose without creating the charge of being anti-Semitic. (I do not suggest that anti-Semitism has completely disappeared from this earth or that the Jews ceased to be Jews altogether. But there has been a slow change of climate.) Among shortages in the post-war world there was a pressing shortage of New Jews. Even in this respect, some nations are better off than others. Some white nations have black minorities (or even majorities). Some black nations have white minorities, others have immigrants of various colours, others again have refugees from Vietnam, Pakistan, Bangladesh, Algeria, Uganda etc. The Swiss have their guest workers and nothing else.

The technique — in all cases — is simple. (1) Bring in a large number of people when they are needed and subsequently complain that they are there. (2) Push them into inferior jobs (jobs which the natives refuse) and then complain that they are inferior; the jobs they do are clear evidence of that. (3) Keep them down and condemn them for being incapable of rising. (4) Deprive them of education and condemn them for being uneducated. (5) Force them into over-crowded houses and condemn them for creating slum conditions. (6) Condemn them for being different: a grave offence, since your own behaviour and attitudes are so obviously the right ones. (7) And finally reject them because of language difficulties. If a Turk or an Albanian speaks less fluent Schwitzerdeutsch than a child from Appenzell, this is a clear indication that he is not much good.

This is the standard recipe for creating scapegoats and — *mutatis mutandis* — has been for thousands of years. Scapegoats are as necessary for psychological survival as shelter is for physical survival. So I fail to understand why we persecute our scapegoats instead of loving them and being grateful to them.

Another question which has puzzled me for a long time is the wild fascination of the *North*. Why do people always look down upon those who live to the immediate south of them? Germans look down upon Swiss Germans; Swiss Germans look down upon Swiss Italians; Swiss Italians look down upon North Italians; North Italians upon South Italians; South Italians upon Sicilians; Sicilians upon Maltese; Maltese upon Arabs; Arabs upon black Africans. Luckily there are no Eskimos at the South Pole, because who could they look down on? They would be psychological cripples.

Swiss nationalists, naturally enough, rationalise their xenophobia. First they protest against the charge: they are not xenophobic, they are liberal and broad-minded people. But Switzerland is a small country and the presence of about one million foreigners (about 600,000 workers plus their families) causes *überfremdung* (over-alienation, i.e. loss of the country's national character). A million temporary visitors called tourists, who bring in money, cause no danger of *überfremdung*; it is the million temporary visitors who earn money and send a lot of it out who are dangerous. The nationalist goes on to say that these foreigners put strong pressures on schools and social services. They stick together and create alien pockets, instead of integrating (but they are prevented from integrating; the Swiss naturalisation laws are among the stickiest in the world). The *gastarbeiter* (the charge goes on) create a housing shortage by their sheer number, and push all prices up.

Constant and lengthy discussion of these problems in the press and at political meetings achieves the desired aim: separation into 'them' and 'us'. We, of course, are the good ones, more settled, more decent and altogether superior. And we are also tolerant and noble, we bear our cross with dignity — although not without a deep sigh — and let the Bosnians and Sicillians go on cleaning our lavatories.

Apart from the Italians, the *gastarbeiter* are not properly organised so they can be pushed around. The Italians *are* well organised which is a further charge against them. *Gastarbeiter* — desperate and ignorant

the gastarbeiter № 1200

people in many cases — are easy prey to Communist and other extremist propoganda, thus another charge is born; all these road-sweepers, waiters and petrol pump attendants endanger Swiss democracy.

I do not wish to exaggerate the economic and political struggle over the *gastarbeiter*. The majority of the Swiss population are sober and tolerant people — otherwise they could not have created that magnificent little country — and the agitation is kept up by a minority of jingoes and neurotics (with perhaps just a few dozen genuinely worried, decent men thrown in). But one or two points should be raised.

About one million Swiss live abroad — almost exactly the number of *gastarbeiter* in Switzerland. The leaders of various national groups in Switzerland often ask the question: do these Swiss cause *überfremdung* abroad?

Another point is about *überfremdung* itself: is the Swiss way of life in real danger? I have my doubts. I should say the same about the English or Turkish way of life, too. And the Bosnian way of life, which Bosnian immigrants to Switzerland are in danger of losing. Perhaps there is an inherent virtue in folk-dancing and yodelling, but these can always be — already are —preserved as museum pieces. Otherwise life is change and there is nothing wrong in change and natural evolution. We all do two things simultaneously: maintain that our way of life is the best in the world and then complain about our lives. When colour gets into the picture, people tend to lose their senses. What if this or that country — say Britain — becomes coffee-coloured in twenty-five or fifty years? What indeed, apart from the fact that we should be a nicer colour?

It may or may not be true that Great Britain is going to the dogs, but as we are a nation of dog-lovers it would not matter much if we did. Nor does it matter if our skin becomes a little darker in the process. It matters even less if Italian and other South-European influences make the Swiss a little livelier, more colourful, noisier, more argumentative and generous, while the Swiss, in turn, make these South-Europeans a little more sedate, dignified, reliable and sober. If we look at our role on this earth, aren't we all just guest workers?

Merci Vielmals

However deep your affection for the Swiss, neither charity nor bias can go so far as to persuade you that their language — Schwitzerdeutsch — is melodious and soothing to the ear. Its gutteral sounds recall Dutch; its distorted German reminds you of broken Yiddish; and the general effect reminds you of gargling during a bad attack of tonsilitis. When you meet a ravishing Swiss girl — and there are plenty of them about — you gasp with admiration: but as soon as she opens her mouth and those regurgitative noises commence it is as though the Venus of Milo were to belch suddenly in public. One cannot imagine the Mona Lisa speaking Schwitzerdeutsch.

It is not only the German language that is being crucified and tormented in Switzerland. The Swiss version of French, as spoken and written in Bernese officialese, is a special language of its own, usually referred to as *Français fédéral*.

Then the mixed areas go a step further and Germanize Gallic words, expressions and phrases, and vice versa. You travel through a great number of villages ending with 'wil' which is, of course, the Germanised version of 'ville'. Or they simply let the two languages mix in the most staggering way — the expression *'merci vielmals'* being a fair example of this unnatural progeny. The three* federal languages raise a great many problems, too: for

*Four, strictly speaking: see next chapter.

instance — to mention only one of these — Switzerland was once compelled to maintain a television service in Italian for 7,000 viewers when 700,000 would scarcely have been an adequate figure to pay for such a service. But it is out of the question for Switzerland to have television in German, but not in French and Italian.

Whatever the Swiss may do with the federal languages, and they do quite a lot, Schwitzerdeutsch is the real, national language of Switzerland.

At first, I cherished misplaced admiration for the intelligence and common sense of the Swiss in these matters. Speaking in Schwitzerdeutsch but writing in Hochdeutsch (proper German — the Kaiser's German, so to say) seemed an excellent compromise between having a language of one's own and not having one. The Dutch, a small nation with their own language — very similar to Plattdeutsch or North-Western German — may be satisfying their national pride but this lands them with a lot of problems: their national language, although it is hardly more than a German dialect, brings them all the troubles of linguistic isolation. The Swiss — I thought — speak their own language but write German; in other words, they have isolation when they want it but they communicate in one of the great languages of the world when it is communication, not isolation, that they want.

Later I understood that my whole conception was based on a mistake. Schwitzerdeutsch is not really a language; it is simply a conspiracy.

This became clear to me when I was staying near Altdorf with a friend who told me of an isolated hotel, beautifully situated up in the mountains, where one could spend a few days in real solitude. It was a place, I was assured, where the Swiss themselves went for their holidays. Normally I do not seek such places; I do not want to go off the beaten track: I want the beaten track and want people around me, the more and the noisier the better. But for one reason or another — I think I wanted to finish writing something — I decided to spend a few days in this hotel, so I rang up to book a room. I was told, politely but firmly, that there was no room. When I mentioned this to my friend, he smiled.

'Did you speak German to them?' he asked.

'Of course,' I replied. 'I cannot expect them to speak English.'

'They speak better English than you do,' said my friend, 'But that's not the point.'

He phoned again, spoke in Schwitzerdeutsch, explained that I, though a foreigner, was a friend of his, and booked a room for me. I found the hotel practically empty. But if you try to book a room in German, it is always full up.

Still later, when I got to know Switzerland better, I realized that the conspiracy of Schwitzerdeutsch works against the Swiss, too.

A Swiss friend of mine married a charming American girl and took her to live in his home town of Schwyz. The girl — I shall call her Susie — accomplished the rare feat of learning Schwitzerdeutsch without a trace of an accent. Her achievement was the more admirable in that she did not speak one word of German.

'I don't want to be regarded as a foreigner in my

husband's country — well, in my own country, that is,' she explained.

A few years later they moved to Zürich, a few miles away. I went to visit them and one day I went shopping with Susie, to the market. To my astonishment she spoke nothing but English to the barrow-boys and street traders, and when they couldn't understand she used sign-language. Driving home I asked her, 'What happened? Have you forgotten your Schwitzerdeutsch?'

She did not answer for a long time. Then she said bitterly, 'There is no such language as Schwitzerdeutsch. I thought there was, but the joke was on me, I guess. There is Zürcherdeutsch, there is Baslerdeutsch, there is Schwyzerdeutsch; and there is St Gallendeutsch. And five dozen other deutsches. When I started to use the language I learned in Schwyz, as soon as I got to Zürich all these good people started nudging each other with their elbows or exchanging knowing looks. I wasn't speaking Zürcherdeutsch. I was a wretched foreigner. Almost an enemy. I am better off with English. . .'

The Fourth Language

You may make fun of a man's country, family, sex-life, religion but not of his language. You may, of course, make *jokes* about a man's language but you must take it basically seriously. 'Fatherland' has become a rather awkward and embarrassing word in the civilised west; but people all over the world, from Belgium through India and from Ceylon to Montreal are prepared to cause riots, anarchy, explosions and, indeed, lay down their lives in defence of their language. It is natural that this should be so. 'Fatherland' is an artificial concept — frontiers can change so easily — and is too often and blatantly abused by politicians. But language becomes part of you, language is one of the main formative factors of your character and thought. Almost my only remaining link with Hungary is the language, my mother tongue, a clumsy, barbaric, agglutinative language, maybe, but dear to me and as much a part of me as my right arm.

I have found it necessary to make these introductory remarks before turning to Switzerland's fourth official language, the Rhaeto-Romansch. I cannot take anything *really* seriously — this is my great weakness and perhaps even greater strength — but I want to make it clear that I am treating this subject with respect.

If Switzerland is one of the largest countries of the world, it follows that Romansch is one of the world's greatest languages, which makes certain comparisons rather puzzling. The English-speaking population of the world is admittedly larger. But take India, for example. Kannada is one of the major languages of India but few non-Indians or non-experts have ever heard of it. Yet, 17½ million people speak that language — more than double the total population of Switzerland, and 350 times as many as speak Romansch. Garwhali is one of the minor Indian languages, only 800,000 people speak it, i.e. only sixteen times as many as Romansch. The truth is that there are altogether about 50,000 Romansch speaking people in the world, mostly in the Canton Grison of Switzerland. Fifty thousand is about half the population of Cambridge. Yet: while people in East Cambridge understand people from West Cambridge, and people talking the East Garwhali dialect easily understand West Garwhali, Romansch consists of five distinct dialects, and the speakers of each one are unintelligible to the speakers of the others. An Engadinian will understand a Sursilvanian even less than a Yorkshireman from the East Riding will understand another Yorkshireman from the West Riding, and that is saying quite a lot.

Engadinian has more affinity to Italian, Sursilvanian to German, I was told. But look at the titles of two journals: *Fögl Ladin* written in Engadinian sounds like a German dialect while *Gasette Romontscha* sounds vaguely Italian. (In fact '*Fögl*' derives from the Latin *folium*, so is quite un-German – just to make it a bit more complicated.)

Romansch seems to be extremely rich in yet another way. The large Oxford Dictionary consists of four fat volumes. A comprehensive dictionary of the Romansch language is being prepared now, and if the present rate of progress is maintained it will not take more than about another two hundred years to complete it. Leading etymologists have compiled *six* huge volumes up to now, but they have only reached the letter *G*.

Rhaeto-Romansch, until the Gothic invasion of Rome, was spoken in Raetia Prima and Raetia Secunda, in other words on today's frontier where German and Italian are spoken. The language derives from a kind of Latin cockney, spoken by the legionarics of Tiberius and Drusus (who subjugated Raetia). Other ancient accounts describe the language as a variety of Etruscan.

In any case, the language has gloriously survived and in 1938 became the fourth official language of Switzerland, next to German, French and Italian. There are fifty-five periodicals published in Romansch, but no daily paper, the nearest to it being an Engadinian newspaper published twice a week. There is an active society for the Promotion of the Romansch language and their Union of Writers has fifty members. It may be disputed whether William Shakespeare is, or is not, the greatest of English writers but it is generally acknowledged that Andri Peer is the greatest Romansch writer. Shakespeare's output is better known; Peer's position is safer. He is a kind and knowledgeable man, now living in Winterthur, near Zürich; a teacher, a prophet, an apostle, etymologist and high priest of Romansch.

'Our children go round on March 1, ringing bells and thus chasing winter away. They also greet the New Year.'

The Roman New Year, to be sure. We have added two months at the beginning of the calendar, but absent-mindedly kept the names of September, October, November and December — meaning seventh, eighth, ninth and tenth month — for the ninth, tenth, eleventh and twelfth months respectively. Romansch children know better: March 1 is still New Year to them.

Romansch being one of the national languages of Switzerland, laws and a lot of official pronouncements must be printed in it. There are Romansch radio programmes, broadcast at Chur, in all five dialects (adding up to only a few hours a day). Television broadcasts are even more modest: one hour in every three weeks, although there is an extra two or three minutes for children every Saturday.

The language is studied and nursed with a great deal of love and devotion. New technical words are invented, scientific phrases are coined, just as they were in Hebrew not so long ago. Is it a difficult language? One cynical German who has learnt it, told me: 'It is not simple but not too difficult for a German. An intelligent German learns it in six months. But a *really* intelligent German does not learn it at all.'

The Swiss, who are not madly keen on squandering their money, spend Frs. 700,000 a year on the Rhaeto-Romansch language, and another Frs. 200,000 on that gigantic dictionary. It would be much simpler, of course, if all the 50,000 Romansch-speaking people spoke one language instead of five. Efforts have been made to unify the language and to convert it into a kind of Romansch Esperanto. The suggestion has been rejected with scorn. In any case it would have only added a sixth language to the existing five.

'Arabs will love Israelis findly before Engadinian will be reconciled with Sursilvanian,' an informant told me, with eyes flashing.

There was one moment in history when the Rhaetians — small nation though they may be — stepped right into the forefront of history. The Rhaetians of today are pious and devout Christians but they tell you with immense pride that it was Rhaetian legionaries who crucified Jesus.

'We were lucky,' someone commented. 'As a result of that act, the world persecuted Jews. Nobody ever persecuted Rhaetians.'

Well, too late now.

On Mountains

Even the most superficial observer is bound to notice sooner or later that there are mountains in Switzerland; and mountains — as man has been aware from the earliest times — are great shapers of character. Swiss life has been a wonderful and, on the whole, successful struggle against the hardships of nature. Today, if you arrive by excellent roads at a solitary inn at a height of 4,000 metres and you find you cannot get the sort of cheese or brand of beer you are used to — only six other kinds — you grumble; and the Swiss proprietor will cast down his eyes in shame.

It is the congestion and bustle of urban life that makes people suspicious and sharp-witted. The men of the mountains trust each other and have plenty of time to think their problems over or, to put the same idea a shade less politely: not even their greatest admirers would allege that the Swiss as a nation are particularly witty or quick on the uptake. When you go into a restaurant (in certain districts) and sit down at a table, a girl will come and ask you what you want. You tell her that you want to eat something. She had to establish this first, since people so frequently go to restaurants for so many different reasons. Some go there to bathe; others to skate; again others to write poetry. But as soon as you have told her that you personally have come to eat, she sees your point and she may bring you the menu. Then again she may not, if she forgets.

Once a friend of mine had a large piece of cake in a *confiserie*, which he greatly enjoyed. He asked the waitress, 'Do you have any more of this cake?'

The girl replied, 'Yes, we have,' and walked away.

But she must have had second thoughts about this because about two minutes later she came back and asked my friend: 'Do you want to see it?' She looked proud of herself for having fathomed the deep meaning of his query.

The urban Swiss, while fully aware of this phenomenon, claim that it is only the Bernese who are so exceptionally slow-witted and, indeed, there are innumerable jokes about the slow-mindedness of the Bernese. The following quip is often repeated.

'What is this?' (they ask you). 'Bum . . . (a minute's pause) . . . bum . . . (a minute's pause) . . . bum . . . (a minute's pause) . . . bum . . .'

If you haven't already guessed, it is a Bernese machine-gun.

The Bernese themselves laugh at these jokes good-heartedly, repeat them (missing the point here and there), and shrug their shoulders.

'We are slow-witted,' a Bernese official told me, 'because we are mountain peasants and not New York gossip columnists. The valleys limit one's horizons. We don't see far. And our slow-wittedness is, of course, a piece of great good luck for Switzerland. Do you think it is simply coincidence that Berne is the capital of Switzerland? Of course not. We are not excitable, we do not hurry into things; we ponder over matters and the eternity of the mountain tops govern all our decisions. If Switzerland were ruled by the foxy traders of Zürich or the wits of Basle, we should have ten times as many troubles, quarrels and disputes with others as we have now.'

Mountain people are not too chatty, not too communicative, and always on their dignity. In some mountain villages funerals are the main festive occasions. Part of the funeral ceremony is a collection: everybody has to throw a ten-centime piece into the box and may take in exchange a ten-centime cigar. Some of the aged poor cannot afford this money for cigars. In other communities in other lands they would probably be given the cigars free. But charity is the ugliest of all virtues and it is so humiliating. So these old people are allowed to throw an old button into the collection box and they get real cigars in exchange. Everyone knows it is buttons they put in; and they know that everyone knows. Yet the ritual survives because the concept of human dignity survives. Real dignity based on a sham — can anything be kinder, more human than that?

Switzerland is perhaps the last remaining country in the world (with the exception of Britain) where quality is still valued and good craftsmanship appreciated. Modern civilization is that of the assembly line and the cheap department store; of mass-production; and I am an enthusiastic supporter of this in all its forms. I revere the firm of Marks and Spencer in Britain, which has made it possible for every shop-girl and factory-worker to dress and look like a duchess; Marksandspencerism has done more for the equality of the human race than Marxism. Nevertheless, pride in one's work, in craftsmanship — the appreciation of something good simply because it *is* good and beautifully made — is a virtue which I don't like to see slowly dying out. And it's not dying out in Switzerland. That does not mean, however, that the Swiss are old-fashioned. Oh no!

If you have ever attempted to climb a mountain, you know that new panoramas and vistas open before you every minute. The mountaineer's horizon may be limited in the valleys; but his view is a constantly varying one and he is used to novelty and change. Indeed, the otherwise conservative and old-fashioned Swiss love everything new, simply for the sake of novelty; they will try everything once; there is no country which is farther away from America in some respects; and no country which is nearer, in others. When I was in Switzerland in the early sixties we read in the newspapers that the first electric computer was being installed in Holland, another small and rich West-European country. The Swiss could hardly believe this. They had at least a hundred computers already: even medium-sized firms had bought them, just for the hell of it, just to see what these things are really like. Packaging is a major art in Switzerland and the amount of new ideas and charm that goes into making up parcels never fails to stagger English visitors. One could say about quite a few matters: what Basle is doing today, London will be doing tomorrow. But London is not so quick in learning. What Basle is doing today, London will be doing — perhaps — next week or next month, with cautious and suspicious restraint. I stayed in a new hotel in Basle: everything was push-button and the last word in modernity. There were red, green, and yellow lights indicating and sometimes fulfilling all your possible and impossible desires. You had your own private safe in each room and you could have your own private aeroplane chartered by the hotel if you so wished. I did not happen so to wish, but I thought nostalgically of English country hotels where the procedure is as follows: if you want something, you push the button marked 'chambermaid', wait five minutes — and then get it yourself.

And finally, the men of the mountains are tough and

rugged, too. I do not say that every Swiss commercial traveller is a William Tell. But the amount of work, endurance, courage, and sheer, mulish stubbornness that must have gone into turning rugged and rocky Switzerland into the modern Paradise it is must make the Pyramids of Egypt blush. There is a Swiss joke about the toughness of the Niedwalden people and it is, in a way, characteristic of the whole nation. A Niedwalden soldier who was taking part in some old-fashioned military exercise was hit by an arrow which pinned him to a tree, so that he could not free himself or even move for nine hours. At last he was found by a comrade of his (a Zürcher merchant) who asked him with sympathy, 'Does it hurt?' The man replied, 'Only when I laugh.'

On the Decline
of Yodelling

One Swiss art which is misunderstood by the world at large is yodelling. The world fails to realise that yodelling is the result of some regrettable physical draw-back and it started as a throat-disease. The Swiss have many great characteristics but, as I ventured to point out before, their language (or dialect?) Schwitzerdeutsch is not the loveliest and/or most melodious of tongues. Indeed, it is maintained by some scientists, that Schwitzerdeutsch is not a language but a throat-disease itself. Whether Schwitzerdeutsch caused the

throat-disease or the throat-disease caused Schwitzerdeutsch I am not competent to say. But the diseased throat is there and it is, undoubtedly, responsible for the art of yodelling.

In my researches I found that no one can yodel in a minor key. I have tried it myself; it is just not possible. I have also found, to my amazement, that yodellers, far from being kept out of foreign lands by tricks, ruses or strict immigration laws, are actually invited — for example to the United States — in large groups to give what they call concerts. It is hard to believe that these yodelling groups appear on the stage, are listened to by enraptured crowds and are actually paid cash for their performance.

Yodelling, however, is (I am informed) a declining art. The reason for this is that Swiss cows are becoming more sophisticated. Yodelling began as a means by which shepherds called their cows in the mountain rain and fog. Old-fashioned Swiss cows heard the shepherds and *went in the direction of the sound*. Sophisticated, modern cows hear the yodelling and run away.

Swiss cows seem to be more musical than some foreign concert-goers, hence the decline of yodelling.

How to Avoid
Winter Sports

Whenever I go to Switzerland in the winter, my chief problem is how to avoid winter sports. It is not an easy task. Dangers lurk in every corner. In November or so, the whole country is transformed into one vast — well, not so terribly vast — ski-run, and few of your kind and hospitable Swiss friends seem able to grasp that your main purpose in life is not to run down a mountain slope at fifty miles an hour as if you were a sixty-horse-power motor-car with faulty brakes.

The railways cease to carry any other goods but skis; and the countryside is transformed into a white infinity, broken only by ski-lifts, carrying small, blue figures and their strange equipment. Whoever is not actually ski-ing, has just finished ski-ing, or is just about to go out ski-ing — and that applies to the ski-lift operator, the railway conductor, the waiter in your hotel, and also to that elderly chambermaid who you thought could hardly walk. You were right. She can hardly walk; but she can ski. 'Ski-ing' nowadays does not mean — at least for a large number of people — just ski-ing in the old sense of the word, but *langlaufen*, the long, endless, exhausting run from valley to valley. I suppose this is one of those modern virility tests. People want to prove their sexual virility almost everywhere: they move about like athletes; they drive long-nosed, fast sports cars like madmen; they run miles and miles on skis. There is one place where many of them fail to prove their sexual virility: in bed. But if they could do that, where would the dealers of sports cars and where would *langlaufen* be?

Well, perhaps I am exaggerating. So let's return to ski-ing. Those few people who are not ski-ing are busy skating, tobogganing, moutaineering, curling, or are out on a run of ski-joring.

If I am so keen to avoid winter sports, the reader

might — not unreasonably — ask, why do I go to Switzerland in winter? The first answer is that I usually have some other business to attend to; secondly, I love Switzerland in the winter, just as in any other season; thirdly, I am addicted to my own private winter sport — that is: avoiding ski-ing. Believe me, it needs much more determination and skill not to ski in Switzerland than to *langlaufen*.

My aversion to ski-ing is purely personal. I am not too much of a duffer in sports that depend largely on one's hands (such as tennis, golf, boxing, or preferably darts, table-tennis and billiards) but I am utterly and ridiculously hopeless in all sports in which you have to rely on your feet. Ever since my earliest youth I have been at war with my feet — and my feet have always won. They have defeated me regularly. For eleven years I went skating; one day my younger brother joined me and I was deeply moved to see that after one single afternoon's practice he was a much better skater than I was after eleven years. That was the end of my career on ice.

Or rather the end of it, with the exception of curling. Curling is a game the Swiss play as a breather between a giant slalom and a round on skates, or whenever they can spare a little time between tobogganing and joring. The game consists of pushing two metal hot-water bottles about on the ice — a pastime which rather suits my skill and temperament. Further than that I am not prepared to go.

Being unable to do something myself has never deterred me from giving advice and instruction to others, so I shall now tell you what you are to do if you are still determined to ski.

(1) First of all, you must join a ski school. If you are a beginner, the teacher will convince you in the first lessons that, however long you live, never in your life will you be able to learn how to ski. If you are a more advanced pupil, the first lessons will recall and confirm these early impressions. You will be ordered to make clumsy and undignified motions which you could perform with ease and grace if your skis were not in your way; yet you are not allowed to take them off. Further, whenever you look round, you will meet maliciously amused eyes of people like me — who watch from the windows of a comfortable hotel lounge or a well-heated car and derive great entertainment from your sufferings. Do not be put off by all this. In a few days you will be surprised to see that you have made great progress and are ready for further suffering and vicissitudes.

There are, as a rule, ten or so people in the ski class and all the ski teachers keep reassuring you that fees are miserably, even shamefully low. I have yet to meet a pupil who was really ashamed to pay his fees because he found them too low, but I believe they are certainly not ruinous.

(2) Every day you must do some shopping. As most people — whether in Switzerland in winter, or at summer sales in Knightsbridge — prefer, at the bottom of their hearts, shopping to ski-ing, this part of the holiday is not regarded as a hardship by anyone. I have never met a skier who had all he (or, even more often, she) needed and who did not dash out to buy various items at least twice a day. One either needs different boots, or another pullover, thinner or thicker gloves, a wind-proof jacket, a pair of ear-flaps, or at least — if one cannot think of anything better and more expensive — a pair of new sunglasses. All this, of course, besides the purchase of watches, chocolate, souvenirs, cameras, precision instruments, etc.

(3) After a few days, when the beginner can already move, you must decide what sort of ski-ing you want to do. You will probably take a train, a tram, a funicular, or a ski-lift to reach one peak or another. You may reach the first peak by bus (three francs), the second by funicular (five francs), the third by a cog-wheeled railway (six francs), the fourth by ski-lift (eight francs), and the fifth by cable-railway (ten francs). Sometimes there is a sixth peak, too; they shoot you up there by cannon at the modest price of twelve francs. (Half the fare returnable if you do not arrive in one piece.) Most people seem to dote on these journeys. I have seen quite a number of them who make eight or nine such journeys a day: as soon as they reach the bottom of a run on skis, they start off up again. They carry time-tables in their pockets and work out complicated connections between cog-railway and ski-lift, so as to outdo the man who sits next to them at supper.

(4) The dangers, however, should not be over-estimated. Before writing this, I met in my club a Swiss

friend, a passionate skier, whose brother is a doctor, and I asked him to tell me something about the dangers of ski-ing. 'It is nonsense to call ski-ing dangerous,' he said. 'Only an infinitesimal proportion of people come to grief and the great majority have no trouble whatever. Nevertheless,' he added thoughtfully, 'Swiss doctors are apt to complain. They are always busier in the winter than they would like to be and that, unfortunately, interferes with their own ski-ing.'

Always carry money in your ski pants.

An English friend of mine broke his leg on a fast slope and although many people passed by, they were running so fast that no one noticed him. At last a girl, a beginner, appeared on the scene, promised to send help and she did. A Swiss gentleman appeared, after a further half hour, with a sleigh. He took out a notebook – my friend still lying in the snow, with a broken leg – and asked him his name, nationality, which hotel he was staying in etc, and put everything down in a little book. Then he said:

'A hundred francs, please.'

My friend paid up, upon which he was placed on the little sleigh and taken to hospital, with great skill and efficiency. The Swiss gentleman was right, of course. Several people had failed to pay him. They want all the fun, free of charge.

(5) If you are really good, soon nothing will be steep, long and fast enough for you. You will find the 3,300 feet of Engelberg ridiculous, the 6,000 feet of the Jochpass not quite up to your standards, St Moritz not steep enough for your liking, the ten miles from Davos to Küblis too short, and even the run from Gornergrat to Zermatt – a five and a half mile descent in about eight minutes – a trifle slow. You need not despair. There is always ski-joring, a sport which has taken enormous strides in the last decade. In olden days, not too

ferocious Swiss horses pulled people on skis across the
ice at Arosa and St Moritz. Then the American GIs
arrived on the scene after the war and motorized this
sport in no time, by using jeeps and lorries. Even this,
however, was soon found too dull. So nowadays they are
experimenting with ordinary aeroplanes: the plane runs
on the ice and you hang on behind. Should it take off,
do not forget to let go of the ropes, Even the tougher
kind of sportsman finds it a little irksome crossing
Switzerland hanging from a plane. But even if the plane
does not take off, a word of warning is found necessary in connection with this new craze. A Swiss guide-
book I have in front of me soberly remarks about ski-
joring-cum-aeroplanes: 'The average tourist may not
have the necesssary skill to participate in this sport.' I
wonder. I have never met an average tourist — at least,
not in Switzerland and after a week's ski-ing — who
admitted that he lacked the skill for anything under the
sun.

If you are looking for even tougher assignments, the
only thing you can do is join the Swiss army. In the
course of their training, Swiss soldiers race over the
middle part of *La Haute Route*. It takes twenty-four
hours non-stop, and I have yet to meet the ski-ing
enthusiast who would not find that *langlaufen* run tough
enough.

On Food

I used to love the famous Swiss soup *Kirschsuppe*. This was because I thought for years that they made it with *Kirsch* and so great is the power of suggestion I used to get quite tipsy on it. Then I learnt that they made it with *Kirsch* the fruit (cherries – I'd noticed them floating about, come to think of it), not *Kirsch* the liqueur. Well, it's still a good soup – and they must have got it from us Hungarians because we invented cherry soup. So I still love *Kirschsuppe*, but with a calmer passion.

In Switzerland many of the girls are as strong and beautiful and many of the men as lean and athletic as any to be seen anywhere in the world; but you can also see as many fat people as in the most sedentary countries of Europe. Quite a few Swiss are worried about their obesity and devote much ingenuity to finding reasons for it. They will give you a great many scientific answers, but only a few of them will hit on the unscientific explanation: because they eat too much. A slice of apple tart in Switzerland is a foot across, a portion of cheese reminds you of the whole cheese-counter in the average English grocer's; and they eat piles of whipped cream. They are always darting off to their excellent confiseries on the slightest provocation and their purpose is not to abstain from sweet, sugary, and creamy things. A worried Swiss lady once told me, 'I don't know why I am still gaining weight. . . . Honestly, I eat only half the amount of whipped cream I used to. . . .'

Swiss restaurants, too, make universal use of a shrewd trick to entice you into an early grave through over-feeding. They have a cunning habit of serving only *half* of your portion at once. You fail to notice this because half a portion in Switzerland looks like a whole portion anywhere else. So you eat your share, with some difficulty because even half is more than enough, and then along comes the waitress, all smiles, and dishes out the other half. If you are as weak a character as I am, you eat that, too.

Swiss food, on the whole, is good and healthy, but, I think, the Swiss *cuisine* cannot compete with the *finesse* of the French. I am, however, one of the greatest living connoisseurs in sausages, which I regard as one of the supreme creations of the human race. Now the Austrians and the Bavarians are no mean sausage nations by any standards, but the Swiss excel them all, by virtue of a giant sausage called the *schüblig*. What Shakespeare is among writers, the *schüblig* is among sausages. A nation which gave the *schüblig* to undeserving humanity is a nation of giants, and must be forgiven anything, including its winter sports; and including its impudence in being a tiny people which yet sets a shining example to the whole world on how to behave normally; how to live well; how to act sensibly in a mad world; how to hate friends and neighbours, and to love humanity — which, if you come to think of it, deserves neither their love nor their *schüblig*.

Liechtenstein:
Small-Power Politics

Liechtenstein is only the third smallest state in the world: both Monaco and the Vatican beat her hands down. She consists of sixty-five square miles: if they were really square, each side would be just over eight miles long. The Concorde would take less than half a minute to fly across her widest expanse. The Duchy of Luxemburg is a veritable giant compared with Liechtenstein, and Switzerland, the vast, dreaded and respected protecting power, is almost 250 times as large.

Switzerland, I ought to add in haste, must not be accused of imperialism. Till the end of World War One, Liechtenstein was under the protection of Austria and it was not without difficulty that she escaped from this embrace. She lies between Switzerland and Austria and it was not Switzerland but Liechtenstein that was anxious to conclude a treaty of customs union. In this Liechtenstein succeeded, at last, in 1924; and so this sole remnant of the Holy Roman Empire — the last of several hundred principalities — managed to save its life and independence and remain a sovereign state. Having learnt her lesson, Liechtenstein became so cautious that during World War Two she forbade her territory even to the soldiers of her treaty-partner, Switzerland whose duty it was to defend her. So the unique situation arose that even Liechtenstein's own soldiers were kept out of the country, surely a new concept of super-neutrality.

Liechtenstein is unique among the countries of the world in quite a few respects. She has no daily newspaper (the *Liechtensteiner Volksblatt* appears four times a week and has a circulation of 4,500). Liechtenstein has no towns, only villages — nine altogether — including Vaduz, the capital, population 4,000. The country has no airfield and the capital has no railway station. Liechtenstein is the only land crossed by many international express trains without their slowing down, let alone stopping. Liechtenstein has no army. She is a fully independent state, with sovereignty but no power. An ideal state of affairs.

On top of it all, Liechtenstein holds some world records. (1) She is — proportionately — the most industrialised country in the world. (2) She is the only country which complains of a shortage of lawyers. (3) She is also the only country still at war with Prussia (because after the 1866 Prussian-Austrian war everybody forgot about Liechtenstein having been a belligerent, and through this regrettable oversight no peace-treaty has ever been concluded. It is too late now: Liechtenstein still flourishes, but Prussia is no longer with us). (4) The Prince of Liechtenstein has the largest and most valuable collection of paintings in private hands. Some irreverent tongues add that the Prince is the greatest living art-dealer in the world.

The world knows very little about Liechtenstein. Just a few facts, half of them wrong. It knows that Liechtenstein is a postage-stamp state (which it is not); that it lives on tourism (which it does not): that it is a tax haven (which it is): and that it is one of the few hereditary monarchies with a truly popular ruler (right again).

The world is inclined to treat Liechtenstein as a joke. I, too, must plead guilty on that count, although I, at least, always admitted that Liechtenstein, if a joke, was a very good joke indeed. But such a view, is, in fact, thoroughly unfair. Everything very small is appealing and provokes not only condescension but also paternal (or maternal) feelings in your bosom. So far so good. But Liechtenstein is a sovereign state, in certain respects, in international law, she ranks equal with the United States or the Soviet Union. (But not as far as voting rights in the United Nations are concerned. Switzerland is not a member of the UN, so Liechtenstein is not a member either). Liechtenstein — like all the tiny states — is very beautiful: the wild and unspoilt mountains of the Grison and St Gallen (Eastern Switzerland) and of Voralberg (Western Austria) — which also means of Liechtenstein, sandwiched between the two — are among the most pleasant, if not the most majestic, sceneries of Europe. The Princess asked me one day if I had seen the country. I told her that I knew the south well but that afternoon would be taken to the north. She looked at me, grimaced, and said with astonishment: 'I never knew our country had a "north".' In other words, the size of Liechtenstein is a joke, but it is also the country's pride.

The official language of Liechtenstein is German. The newspapers are printed and all official documents are drawn up in *Hochdeutsch*, high German, but the language actually spoken is *Alemmannic,* an odd mixture of

German, Swiss German and Romansch.

Liechtenstein is represented abroad by Switzerland. She has only one diplomatic representative: in Berne, the capital of Switzerland. The diplomatic corps of Liechtenstein consists of Prince Heinrich, younger brother of the ruling Prince. Switzerland, in turn, maintains no diplomatic representation in Liechtenstein; on the other hand quite a number of states (twenty, to be precise) maintain consuls, honorary or otherwise, in Vaduz: among them Peru, San Marino, Monaco and Brazil. When I enquired why some of these states need consuls in Liechtenstein, I received the perfectly convincing reply: 'Because some people like being consuls.'

Liechtenstein has no currency of its own: the Swiss Franc is legal tender. But she has, as everyone knows, her own postage stamps. Indeed, the Philatelic Section is regarded as one of the most important institutions of the state. It has 96,000 regular persons on its mailing list, i.e. more than four regular foreign stamp-collectors per inhabitant. The United States would need 800 million regular stamp-buying clients (the total population of China?) to equal this. The first stamps were issued in February 1912 and Liechtenstein never looked back since. Last year postage stamps supplied one quarter of the total revenue.

'We may be one of the smallest states but we are one of the greatest philatelic powers,' Herr Hugo Mayer, director of the Philatelic Section remarked. Herr Mayer might have added that Liechtenstein is the only country of the world where you can get a few really good collectors' items for your stamp collection in every grocer's. Should you feel a sudden urge to buy a few rare stamps between four and five in the morning, automatic selling machines will attend to your need.

Liechtenstein's tourism is beset with a serious dilemma. In the early days Liechtensteiners, like many other people, disliked tourists. Most of them still dislike them. This is not just xenophobia but reasoned judgement. There is a tremendous shortage of labour in the country. Industry could not exist without foreign labour. So there is rivalry between industry and tourism: tourism takes away labour from industry. One day the daily influx of foreigners may cease — many people fear — and then tourism will gain in importance. At the moment tourism brings in only two or three per cent of the revenue.

'Liechtenstein is not a truly mondaine place,' the Director of Tourism told me.

This was the understatement of the year. I usually went to bed at 9.30, a late hour in these parts. Most people were already in bed, shoes neatly placed outside the hotel rooms.

'Not a truly mondaine place,' he repeated. 'No casino, no sex, no nakedness. I don't want to transform Liechtenstein into a European Las Vegas.' But surely a *small* casino would not hurt? A few *serious* night-clubs could do it no harm?

Liechtenstein began her career as a Roman Province. Her history books are full of local wars and unknown battles, such as the Appenzeller War, the old Zürich War and the Battle of Bad Ragaz. The most significant of these wars was the Swabian War because, as a result of it, Liechtenstein became a dependency of Austria, in the early sixteenth century. During the Thirty Years War Liechtenstein was ravaged and invaded by among others, the Swedes. The Liechtensteiners, always fond of records, point out that their country marked the southernmost point of the Swedish advance. After the Swedes came Wallenstein; after Wallenstein, Suvarov's Russians.

Once these disastrous years were over Liechtenstein's

history became a mixture of peasant commonsense and good luck. The luck started when Charles of Liechtenstein was elevated to the rank of Prince (actually *before* the war, in 1608). He was determined to be accepted by his fellow princes as an equal. In order to gain a seat and vote in the Diet of the Holy Roman Empire he needed proper estates, and he started a frantic search. The second piece of luck was that two Austrian counts went bankrupt and Charles's descendant, John Adam Andrew, was able to buy their estates, Schellenberg and Vaduz, for 290,000 florins, after the Thirty Years War. Considering today's real estate price, the two estates (which were subsequently given the prince's family name, Liechtenstein) were the bargain of the century.

The Prince and his successors rarely visited Liechtenstein (the present ruler is the first to live permanently in the country). Napoleon liked Prince Johannes of Liechtenstein so much that he turned Liechtenstein into an independent principality and made her a member of the Confederation of the Rhine as a reward for services rendered to him. Prince Johannes, however, liked Napoleon less than Napoleon liked him, turned against the Emperor, fought him in the Battle of Aspern and, after Waterloo, as a reward for his services *against* Napoleon, was permitted to remain independent and become a member of the German Federation. Till the end of World War One Liechtenstein was protected by Austria; after Austria's defeat she became a *protégé* of Switzerland.

Liechtenstein history has achieved yet another — well, not record, but silver medal. The good Prince Johannes II reigned from 1858 till 1928, seventy years all told. This makes him the second longest-reigning monarch of Europe. He is decisively beaten by Louis XIV (seventy-seven years) but is ahead of Francis Joseph of Austria-Hungary (sixty-eight years) and Catherine the Great of

Russia (sixty-seven). Queen Victoria (sixty-three years) is a mere also ran.

Liechtenstein's military history is curious. The army started with five men — not an impressive force by any standards. This was the contingent the country was obliged to provide for the Imperial Austrian Army. Napoleon raised this number to forty and the German Federation to eighty. This rise — from five to eighty — meant a sixteen-fold increase in Liechtenstein military might, unprecedented in the history even of the most savagely militaristic country.

The last war in which Liechtenstein participated was the 1866 Austro-Prussian war. The eighty Liechtenstein soldiers marched off (actually against Prussia's ally, Italy) with banners flying and trumpets blaring. The campaign turned out a Thermopylae in reverse. Far from fighting to the last men, actually more soldiers returned than had left: eighty-one instead of eighty. It is said that an Austrian soldier joined them: he deemed it safer to be with the Liechtenstein contingent. Indeed, they had spent their time in the Stelvio Pass and none had set eyes on the enemy. Two years later Prince Johannes II dissolved the army.

A few years ago, Liechtenstein was very poor and almost entirely an agricultural country, with some minor industries. The manufacture of sausage skins and artificial teeth were the most important among them. Some malicious economists maintained that Liechtenstein's two basic industries were complementary and helped each other: the more one indulged in chewing sausage skins the more artificial teeth one needed in due course.

Those days are over. Now only five per cent of Liechtenstein's inhabitants are engaged in agriculture, and while sausage skins and artificial teeth still flourish (if this be the right word), new and more important industries have sprung up: precision instruments, chemical products, modern fastening systems, central heating apparatus, textiles, vehicle bodies, electrical installations, furniture, machine tools, deep freeze products, canned meat etc. Liechtenstein today exports to eighty-five countries all over the globe and one firm, Barzels, even exported some instruments to the moon. They are ultra-high vacuum specialists and made important contributions to the NASA lunar shot, Apollo 16.

Capital and foreign investments are no problem of Liechtenstein's. She has only one major worry: shortage of labour. In addition to the 7,000 foreign workers living in the country, 2,500 *frontaliers* cross the frontiers daily, mostly from Austria but some from Switzerland. In fact, Liechtenstein is the only country in the world where the Swiss — the Swiss! — appear as *Gastarbeiter*.

One of Liechtenstein's chief industries is, as is well known, the registration of foreign companies. What Panama and Liberia are to the maritime world, Liechtenstein is to international commerce. Thousands of companies sail under the Liechtenstein flag of convenience. Directors need not be resident in the country and there is no income or company tax. All that the holding companies have to pay every year is a tax on capital of 1 per thousand (with a minimum of 400 francs). No names of companies or directors are ever published, this is a part — indeed, a most essential part — of the service. Even the number of the companies registered is a closely guarded secret. Talking to one of the gentlemen in the know, I tried to get the figure out of him. I met a blank wall and failed miserably. In the end, I suggested that the number of foreign firms registered might be as high as 4,000. He found this deliberately low figure so insulting to the honour of Liechtenstein that he blurted out the figure: more than 25,000. That makes more than one holding company per head and more than three and a half holding companies per voter.

It is the holding companies which turn Leichtenstein into a lawyers' paradise. A foreign company must have a Liechtenstein representative and Liechtenstein lawyers have grown so rich that quite a few are supposed to own vast foreign companies registered in Liechtenstein.

Even the official handbook throws up its hands and admits that it would be difficult to explain the intricacies of Liechtenstein politics to a foreigner. It is equally difficult to explain them to a Liechtensteiner. The Patriotic Union has a majority of one over the Progressive Citizens' Party in a Diet of fifteen, and the Government is a coalition. So far so good. The right-wing (government) party, one Member of Parliament remarked, is monarchist, Catholic and bourgeois, while the right-wing (opposition) party is bourgeois, monarchist and Catholic. I asked Dr Alfred Hibe, the Prime Minister: 'How left is your left?' 'Pretty right,' he replied with a disarming grin, obviously joking, but equally obviously speaking no more than the truth. Yet, it is all very simple. Politics in a small state revolve not so much around principles as around personalities. Just as in large states, nowadays. The true difference between the Parties is that one is in, the other is out. A significant enough difference. But Liechtenstein herself proves the case: her political life is as noisy and acrimonious as if the gulf between the parties were unbridgeable.

Small-power politics, as has often been explained to me, has its dangers and pitfalls. Out of Leichtenstein's 21,000 inhabitants one third are foreigners and another 7,000 are women who have no right to vote. That leaves 7,000 voters to elect a Parliament of fifteen. Before the Patriotic Party gained its majority of one, the Progressive Citizens' Party had the same majority: in other words the gain or loss of one single seat may result in a change of government.

But that is not all. That means that 466 voters elect one member of Parliament, consequently a difference of fifty votes — and that only means twenty-five people changing their allegiance — can change the ruling party of the land. That may sound like real democracy but — as a number of Liechtenstein politicians maintain — is, in fact, quite the contrary. In a state where twenty-five votes can sway an election, a large family with seven or eight votes wields tremendous power. The *paterfamilias* in charge may apply for a licence of some sort or another and no government, no ministry, no Prime Minister will dare to refuse him, however unjustified his claim may be. Voters have tyrannical power. As one politician wrily remarked: 'This is the tyranny of the people over bureaucracy. I assure you, sometimes this can be almost as bad as the tyranny of bureaucracy over the people.'

Government House is a two-storey building in the main street of Vaduz. It houses all the ministries and several auxiliary departments. The Ministry of Finance and the Treasury occupy room 26, on the first floor. Next door is the Ministry of Agriculture. Room 19 is a private room for Gentlemen. The Minister of Interior and the Police reside in room 3, on the ground floor. The High Court of Justice, with all its officers and offices takes up room 35 (second floor), the Parliament is in room 39. There is a small annex which houses the State Archives as well as the Government Press and Information Department. The prison is in the basement of the main building.

Both parties are devoted to the monarchy, and to the Prince, Franz Josef II, the last Habsburg ruler in the world (yet another Liechtenstein record). He ascended the throne (but there is no throne) in 1938. He is a shy man in his mid-sixties, a forestry engineer by training. He is impeccably courteous and hospitable, and his serious face often lights up in a kind and warm smile. He was wearing a white turtle-neck pullover, green tweed jacket and grey trousers when I saw him. He is a tall man, with typical Habsburg lips, small moustache and receding hair. He received me in his castle, towering three hundred feet above Vaduz, perching on the beautiful green mountainside. There are always a number of sightseers outside. There are no guards, no uniforms in front of the castle or inside. There is a porter in a small hut who — as I was accompanied by the Head of the Government's Press Department — waved us in without any questions. In the courtyard there were four Mercedes cars, with number plates FL (standing for Fürstentum Liechtenstein, Principality of Liechtenstein), FL 1, FL 2, FL 3 and FL 5. FL 4 was missing. FL 5 was smaller than the rest. The Princess drives around in that one.

We were received by a valet in shirt-sleeves who hurriedly put on his wine-coloured jacket and then looked like an employee of one of those Austrian hotels which try to pose as establishments for hunters. The staff, by the way, number less than ten, all told, for the huge palace: the shortage of labour affects the Prince as much as anyone else.

The castle itself is an ancient building, first mentioned in chronicles in 1322, rebuilt and enlarged many times since those days. It is a comfortable, modern castle as castles go, with central heating and many bathrooms. Thanks to the Princess it is not only a princely palace and a museum, but also a home.

I was shown around the palace. It is a real home but by no means a modest little middle-class home. It has 115 rooms of which forty are in use. It has its own chapel, large but simple, where a retired priest says mass every morning in front of a beautiful fifteenth century altar. It contains an impressive golden statue of St. George, by an unknown mediaeval artist. The castle has no swimming pool but has a large and famous armoury, complete with breastplates, cannons, rifles, flags, torture-instruments, shields, spears and cavalry sabres. And there are antlers, antlers everywhere, in every room, on every wall. The cellar houses the world-famous picture collection – not open to the public – paintings by Van Dyck, Rubens, Franz Hals, Dürer and many others, but no Leonardo any more. The Leonardo was sold to America for more than five million dollars. The Americans had no Leonardo and just *had* to acquire one, at any price.

I was intrigued by the ubiquitous antlers. The truth is that the Prince is not a fervent huntsman. He goes out shooting occasionally but it does not mean much to him. As far as I know he has only one serious hobby: getting away from the tourists.

The Princess is a very different type of person. Born Countess Georgina Wilczek, she married her husband in 1943 and they have five children. She is the typical Austrian Countess, friendly, charming and chatty, a great extrovert with an infectious laugh. She is known as Gina throughout the length and breadth of the land, and she is found irresistible – a judgement easy to share.

I had heard that she was travelling, driving and walking around all by herself in Liechtenstein as well as in Switzerland and Austria, and suggested that she must be fond of a simple, unceremonious life.

'Not at all,' she replied. 'I love pomp and circumstance. Some years ago we paid our one and only state visit with my husband. It was a visit to Switzerland. I just adored the receptions, the state banquets, the red carpets, the ceremony, the processions and the cheering crowds. I was carried away, much more than the people themselves. I had the time of my life. I wish we paid more state visits to many more countries. But we are not invited.'

I was struck by the universal and unquestioning loyalty to the Princely House — an unusual phenomenon in the last third of the twentieth century. But it is real. I talked to a number of people about it and their combined, unanimous, view runs like this:

'We are snobs — like everyone else, all over the world. We prefer to have a real Habsburg Prince rather than some obscure President. Secondly, the Prince is a nice and likeable man and his wife is very much loved. Thirdly, the Prince is not only much better than a President would be, but is also much cheaper. He costs us nothing. When he needs money he sells a Leonardo or something, and he is in funds for years to come.'

The prison, as we know, is in the basement of Government House. One winter night, a former Deputy Prime Minister told me, he was working very late (9.30 or so), and when he decided to go home he discovered with dismay that someone had locked the main door and he could not get out of the building. He started banging on the door, trying to attract the attention of passers-by, but there are no passers-by in the streets of Vaduz on winter evenings at 9.30. At last a sleepy and somewhat irritated man emerged from the cellar, carrying a bunch of keys. He let the Deputy Prime Minister out.

'Who are you?' enquired the Minister.

'I am the prisoner.'

'And you've got the keys?'

'Of course.'

'And what are you going to do now?'

'Go back to my cell and lock myself in.'

Well, what else could he do? Unless he wished to leave his country, he couldn't escape. In Liechtenstein everybody knows everybody and one cannot flee across state frontiers as in the United States. And no one wishes to leave the country, emigration is anathema to the Liechtensteiner. One middle-aged man, who had tried it, told me that he had gone to St Gallen, a Swiss town in the neighbouring Canton. He did well there, became prosperous and, in those days, he could not see much future for himself in Liechtenstein. Yet he came back.

'I was homesick. I couldn't bear it.'

'This devotion to our tiny land is one of the main traits of the Liechtenstein character,' many people assured me. I questioned this statement. *Liechtenstein character*? I had a long argument with one of their leading industrialists. Did he really mean that this tiny segment of Europe had produced a special character? Yes, he did. Well, in what way did it differ from the character of the Swiss of St Gallen or of the Austrians of Voralberg? He smiled and said: 'If you promise that you won't tell anyone, I'll admit it: there is no Liechtenstein character.'

But, on reflection, he was wrong and I, angling for this reply, was wrong, too. There *is* such a thing as the Liechtenstein character. Almost two centuries of independence has bred in the people of Liechtenstein a deep love for their little country. They feel a little different from the rest of humanity living in real, serious countries, even if that difference is no more than a peculiarity. Their love for Liechtenstein is no fierce patriotism, no militaristic menace (a country without an army cannot be very militaristic or very menacing), but it is deep, an affection mingled with a peasant stubbornness expressed in their determination to live their own lives in their own way. Their very smallness shapes their outlook, too. They are rich; successful; independent (perhaps more independent than some larger states: who cares about Liechtenstein? and who wants to hurt a baby?); but they are powerless and pleasantly insignificant. Their land is beautiful, unpolluted, their lives lived at a slower rhythm, at a more civilized pace. We, in New York, in London, in Tokyo, know how to be immense; it is time to study Liechtenstein and learn how to be small.

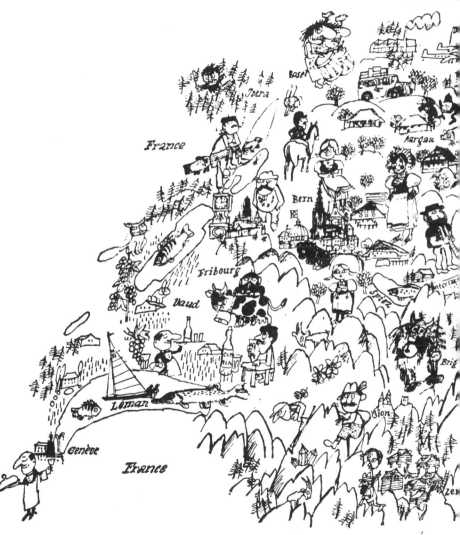